AI Cybersecurity Fundamentals

Protecting Digital Systems in the Age of Artificial Intelligence

By Joe Correa

Published by Live Stronger Faster

This book is for educational and informational purposes only. The author and publisher are not engaged in rendering legal, financial, tax, or other professional advice. Readers should consult a qualified professional before making any financial decisions.

First Edition

Table of Contents

Introduction 5

Chapter 1: What Is AI Cybersecurity and Why It Matters 12

Chapter 2: Human vs Machine Responsibility in AI Cybersecurity 20

Chapter 3: Algorithmic Bias, Manipulation, and Trust in AI Cybersecurity 27

Chapter 4: Data, Training, and the Security of AI Systems 33

Chapter 5: The AI Threat Landscape: How Modern Attacks Are Evolving 39

Chapter 6: Zero-Trust Security and AI Threat Monitoring 44

Chapter 7: AI Malware, Ransomware, and Digital Warfare 52

Chapter 8: AI Privacy, Surveillance, and Data Exploitation 60

Chapter 9: AI Cyber Risk, Compliance, and Digital Forensics 68

Chapter 10: The Future of AI Cybersecurity: Global Cyber War, Autonomous Defense, and Digital Survival 76

Final Thoughts 84

Introduction

Artificial intelligence has quietly become the most powerful force ever unleashed on the digital world, and with that power comes a new kind of vulnerability that most people do not yet fully understand. Every algorithm that makes life easier also creates new attack surfaces, every automation tool that saves time also introduces new security risks, and every intelligent system that learns from data can be manipulated by those who know how to poison, deceive, or exploit it. We now live in an era where cyberattacks are no longer written by human hands line by line but generated, optimized, and executed by machines that can scan, adapt, and strike faster than any security team can react. AI cybersecurity is no longer a niche field or a futuristic concept; it is now the frontline of global digital survival.

For decades, cybersecurity was built around predictable threats. Viruses were coded by people, malware was distributed through known channels, and attacks followed recognizable patterns. Firewalls, antivirus software, and intrusion detection systems were designed to match known signatures and stop familiar techniques. But artificial intelligence has changed the battlefield. Modern cyberattacks are now self-learning, self-modifying, and capable of evolving in real time. AI-powered malware can test millions of variations of an attack until it finds one that slips through defenses. Phishing campaigns are no longer mass-produced with obvious grammatical errors but are now personalized, emotionally intelligent, and almost indistinguishable from legitimate communication. Deepfake audio and video can convincingly impersonate executives, politicians, and family members, making fraud and extortion terrifyingly effective. The rules of cybersecurity have been rewritten.

At the same time, artificial intelligence is also becoming the most powerful defensive tool humanity has ever had. AI cybersecurity systems can analyze vast amounts of network data in real time, identify subtle anomalies that no human could detect, and predict attacks before they fully unfold. Machine learning models can recognize patterns of malicious behavior even when they have never seen that exact attack before. Behavioral analytics can detect insider threats, compromised accounts, and silent intrusions that would otherwise remain invisible for months or years. This dual nature of AI — as both weapon and shield — defines the modern cybersecurity landscape. The same technology that enables unprecedented cybercrime also enables unprecedented protection.

This book begins a professional journey into understanding how artificial intelligence intersects with cybersecurity at every level of modern digital life. Whether you are a business owner protecting customer data, a professional managing corporate networks, a developer building AI-powered products, or simply someone who relies on digital systems to live and work, the security of artificial intelligence affects you directly. AI cybersecurity is not just about protecting servers and databases; it is about protecting financial systems, healthcare records, elections, supply chains, and even personal identity itself. The collapse of digital trust would be as damaging to society as the collapse of financial trust, and AI sits at the center of both.

Understanding AI cybersecurity begins with understanding how artificial intelligence actually works. AI systems are not magical or mystical. They are trained on data, guided by algorithms, and driven by objectives. Every dataset can be poisoned. Every model can be manipulated. Every automated decision system can be tricked if attackers understand how it thinks. Unlike traditional software, AI systems do not behave in fixed, predictable ways. They adapt, learn, and sometimes make decisions that even their creators cannot fully explain. This creates powerful capabilities, but it also introduces new vulnerabilities that did not exist before. Attackers no longer need to break into a system if they can instead influence what the system believes. The rise of AI-driven platforms has also dramatically expanded the attack surface of the internet. Cloud-based AI services, automated customer support bots, recommendation engines, facial recognition systems, voice authentication, and predictive analytics engines are now embedded in nearly every digital platform. Each of these systems processes sensitive data and makes high-stakes decisions. If compromised, they can be used to steal identities, manipulate behavior, bypass security, or launch large-scale automated attacks. AI cybersecurity must therefore protect not only traditional IT infrastructure but also the intelligent systems that sit on top of it.

This series is designed to give you a complete professional understanding of this new digital battlefield. In this first book, you will learn the foundational concepts that everything else is built upon. You will explore what AI cybersecurity actually means, how artificial intelligence changes the threat landscape, and why traditional security approaches are no longer sufficient. You will see how data, algorithms, and automation reshape both attack and defense, and you will gain a framework for thinking about AI security that applies across industries, technologies, and geopolitical boundaries. Without these fundamentals, it is impossible to fully grasp the more advanced topics that follow.

One of the most dangerous myths about artificial intelligence is that it is too complex for ordinary people to understand or influence. In reality, the greatest cybersecurity failures often come from human misunderstanding rather than technical flaws. AI systems do exactly what they are trained to do, but if they are trained on biased, poisoned, or incomplete data, they will make dangerous decisions with total confidence. If they are connected to insecure systems, they will become powerful tools for attackers. If organizations deploy AI without proper security, governance, and monitoring, they create risks that no firewall can fix. AI cybersecurity is therefore not only a technical discipline but also a management, policy, and ethical challenge.

As you move through this book, you will begin to see how artificial intelligence forces a complete rethinking of digital trust. In the past, identity was verified by passwords, documents, and physical presence. Today, identity is increasingly verified by AI systems that analyze faces, voices, behavior, and data patterns. When those systems are compromised, the consequences are devastating. Financial fraud, political manipulation, corporate espionage, and social engineering all become easier, faster, and harder to detect. AI cybersecurity is about defending not just machines but the very concept of who is real, who is authorized, and who can be trusted in a digital world.

This book also lays the groundwork for understanding how AI is reshaping the global balance of power. Nations are now engaged in a quiet but intense cyber arms race, where AI-powered hacking, surveillance, and defense systems determine economic stability, military readiness, and political influence. Corporations that control powerful AI systems hold enormous leverage over markets, data, and digital infrastructure. Criminal organizations now operate at a scale and sophistication that rivals nation-states, thanks to automation and artificial intelligence. In this environment, cybersecurity is no longer just an IT function — it is a matter of national security, corporate survival, and personal safety.

The goal of this introduction is not to scare you, but to awaken you to the reality that the digital world you depend on is undergoing a fundamental transformation. The rise of artificial intelligence makes everything faster, smarter, and more efficient, but it also makes everything more fragile if not properly protected. AI cybersecurity is the discipline that stands between innovation and chaos. It is the field that ensures that progress does not become vulnerability, that automation does not become exploitation, and that intelligence does not become a weapon against its own creators.

As you continue through this series, each book will dive deeper into a specific dimension of this evolving battlefield, from AI-powered hacking to deepfake fraud, from automated cyber defense to privacy and surveillance, from compliance and forensics to the future of global digital warfare. But all of it begins here, with a clear understanding of what AI cybersecurity is and why it matters. This first book gives you the foundation you need to navigate a world where machines think, attackers automate, and security must become just as intelligent as the threats it faces.

Chapter 1

What Is AI Cybersecurity and Why It Matters

Artificial intelligence has permanently transformed the meaning of security in the digital age, turning what was once a battle of human programmers into a confrontation between intelligent machines operating at speeds and scales no human team could ever match. AI cybersecurity is the discipline that exists to protect digital systems, data, and identities from threats that are themselves powered by artificial intelligence. It is no longer enough to simply block known malware or monitor network traffic for suspicious behavior, because modern attacks are now adaptive, automated, and self-improving. AI-driven threats can analyze defenses, find weaknesses, and evolve their methods in real time, making static security tools obsolete almost the moment they are deployed. AI cybersecurity therefore represents a shift from reactive defense to continuous, intelligent protection that learns and adapts just as fast as the attackers.

At its core, AI cybersecurity combines machine learning, behavioral analytics, automation, and predictive modeling to defend against digital threats that are too fast, too complex, and too subtle for traditional tools. Instead of relying on fixed rules or known signatures, AI security systems study how users, networks, and applications normally behave and then detect when something deviates from that baseline. A single unusual login, a strange pattern of data movement, or a slight change in how a system communicates can trigger alerts that reveal an attack long before it becomes destructive. This ability to detect the unknown is what makes artificial intelligence so powerful in cybersecurity, and it is also what makes it so dangerous when used by attackers.

The reason AI cybersecurity matters so deeply is that the modern world is now built on digital trust. Banks trust that online transactions are legitimate, hospitals trust that patient records have not been altered, governments trust that their communications are secure, and individuals trust that the messages they receive come from who they claim to come from. Artificial intelligence sits behind much of this trust, quietly making decisions about credit approvals, identity verification, fraud detection, and access control. When those AI systems are compromised, the consequences ripple through entire economies and societies. A single successful AI-powered attack can manipulate markets, disrupt infrastructure, or destroy lives by stealing identities, draining accounts, or spreading false information at massive scale. Traditional cybersecurity was built for a world where threats were created by people and followed recognizable patterns. Antivirus software looked for known virus signatures, firewalls blocked specific types of traffic, and intrusion detection systems flagged suspicious activity based on predefined rules. But AI-powered attacks do not behave like that. They can generate new malware variants on the fly, test thousands of attack strategies in seconds, and hide inside normal network activity so effectively that they become nearly invisible. This is why AI cybersecurity is not just an upgrade to traditional security but a complete reimagining of how digital defense must work in an intelligent age.

One of the most important aspects of AI cybersecurity is its ability to understand context. A human logging in from a new device might be normal if they are traveling, but it might be a sign of a compromised account if it happens at an unusual time, from an unusual location, with an unusual pattern of behavior. AI systems can analyze all of these variables at once and make probability-based decisions about whether an action is legitimate or malicious. This allows organizations to block attacks without disrupting normal operations, something that older security systems struggled to do. Contextual intelligence is what allows AI cybersecurity to be both powerful and precise.

AI cybersecurity also plays a critical role in defending against modern forms of deception. Deepfakes, synthetic voices, automated chatbots, and AI-generated emails are now used to impersonate executives, trick employees, and steal sensitive information. These attacks succeed not because systems are weak, but because humans are psychologically vulnerable. AI-powered defense systems can analyze voice patterns, writing styles, facial movements, and behavioral signals to detect when something is not real, even when it looks or sounds convincing to a person. This makes AI one of the only tools capable of fighting deception at scale.

Another reason AI cybersecurity matters is the sheer volume of data that modern systems generate. Every click, login, transaction, and message produces information that could reveal a threat, but no human team could possibly analyze it all. AI systems can process this ocean of data in real time, finding subtle correlations and patterns that indicate risk. They can predict which systems are most likely to be attacked, prioritize vulnerabilities, and even automatically deploy defenses before an attacker strikes. This predictive capability turns cybersecurity from a constant state of crisis into a strategic discipline.

The rise of AI has also blurred the line between internal and external threats. Insider attacks, whether intentional or accidental, are now one of the biggest risks to organizations. An employee who clicks on a malicious link or uploads data to an insecure system can trigger a chain reaction that leads to massive breaches. AI cybersecurity systems can monitor behavior inside the organization, detecting when someone's actions deviate from their normal patterns and stopping potential disasters before they unfold. This kind of protection is essential in a world where people and machines work side by side.

Ultimately, AI cybersecurity matters because it protects the foundations of modern life. Our money, our identities, our health, our businesses, and our governments all depend on digital systems that are increasingly powered by artificial intelligence. If those systems are not secure, nothing built on top of them is safe. AI cybersecurity is the invisible shield that allows innovation to continue without turning the digital world into a lawless battlefield. Understanding it is no longer optional for professionals, leaders, or citizens; it is a requirement for survival in the intelligent age.

The Day the Network Learned to Fight Back

In a quiet operations center tucked beneath a glass skyscraper, the city's largest financial network hummed with invisible life as billions of transactions flowed through its servers every hour. Most of the room was dark, lit only by the glow of massive screens that displayed shifting graphs, flowing data, and the subtle pulse of the artificial intelligence system that guarded the entire digital ecosystem. To the people who worked there, it felt almost alive, constantly watching, learning, and adjusting. They called it Sentinel, and it was the last line of defense between the city's economy and chaos.

No one noticed when the first attack began. A single login attempt from an unfamiliar device, followed by a few unusual data requests, slipped quietly into the network. To a human analyst, it would have looked harmless, lost among millions of normal activities. But Sentinel noticed something subtle: the rhythm of the requests did not match any known human behavior. The system flagged the activity, not with an alarm, but with curiosity. It began to watch, silently building a profile of what was happening.

Within minutes, the attack expanded. Automated scripts began probing deeper into the network, testing passwords, mapping systems, and searching for weaknesses. The attackers were using their own artificial intelligence, a machine designed to explore and exploit any opening it could find. It moved faster than any human hacker ever could, adjusting its strategy each time it encountered resistance. But Sentinel was faster. Every probe taught it more about the attacker's methods, and every failed attempt sharpened its defensive model.

As the attackers pushed harder, trying to breach the financial vaults that held millions of customer accounts, Sentinel began to fight back. It rerouted traffic, isolated vulnerable systems, and deployed digital decoys that looked like valuable targets but were actually traps. The attacking AI fell for them, pouring its efforts into breaking into fake databases that revealed nothing of value. With each move, Sentinel learned more about its opponent, refining its predictions and tightening its defenses.

In the operations center, a lone security engineer named Maya watched the unfolding battle with a mix of awe and dread. She had designed parts of Sentinel's learning algorithms, but she had never seen them operate at this level. On one screen, she saw the attacker's strategies being mapped in real time. On another, she saw Sentinel anticipating their next move before it happened. It was like watching two invisible minds playing a high-speed game of chess with the city's economy as the prize.

The attackers made one final push, unleashing a powerful wave of malicious code designed to overwhelm the system. For a brief moment, network traffic spiked, alarms flickered, and Maya felt her heart race. Then Sentinel responded. It absorbed the attack, neutralized the malware, and traced the digital fingerprints back to their source. Within seconds, the threat was contained, the compromised pathways were sealed, and the attackers were locked out completely.

When the network finally settled back into its normal rhythm, the city never even knew how close it had come to disaster. Millions of people went about their day, their money safe, their data secure, unaware that a silent war had been fought and won in the digital shadows. Maya leaned back in her chair, exhausted but relieved. For the first time, she truly understood what AI cybersecurity meant. It was not just software. It was a living, learning defense system that protected the modern world while no one was watching.

Chapter 2

Human vs Machine Responsibility in AI Cybersecurity

As artificial intelligence becomes more deeply embedded into the systems that protect and govern our digital world, one of the most complex and important questions in AI cybersecurity emerges: who is responsible when something goes wrong — the human or the machine? In traditional cybersecurity, accountability was relatively straightforward. A developer wrote code, a security team configured systems, and an organization made policy decisions. When a breach occurred, investigators could trace the failure back to human choices. In the age of AI, however, systems now make autonomous decisions, adapt their own behavior, and execute actions without direct human intervention. This creates a new and often uncomfortable reality in which the line between human responsibility and machine responsibility becomes blurred.

AI cybersecurity systems are designed to detect, predict, and respond to threats faster than any human could. They block logins, isolate networks, shut down accounts, and reroute data in milliseconds. These actions can prevent catastrophic damage, but they can also cause harm if they are wrong. A false positive could lock a company out of its own systems. A misclassified behavior could label an innocent user as a criminal. When these decisions are made by an algorithm, the question of accountability becomes far more complicated than when they are made by a human security analyst.

The truth is that artificial intelligence does not possess moral responsibility in the way humans do. It does not understand right or wrong, fairness or injustice, or the consequences of its actions in a human sense. It simply follows mathematical models trained on data and optimized for specific outcomes. The responsibility for those outcomes ultimately rests with the humans who design, train, deploy, and govern the system. However, because AI systems learn from data and evolve over time, even their creators may not be able to fully predict how they will behave in every situation. This unpredictability makes governance and oversight a central pillar of AI cybersecurity.

One of the most dangerous misconceptions about AI is that it can replace human judgment entirely. In reality, the most effective AI cybersecurity systems are those that operate in partnership with skilled human professionals. Humans define objectives, ethical boundaries, and risk tolerance, while machines execute at scale and speed. When that balance breaks down — when AI is given too much autonomy without oversight or when humans ignore the signals that AI provides

— the result is either reckless automation or missed threats. Responsibility must therefore be shared, structured, and continuously monitored.

Legal systems around the world are still struggling to adapt to this new reality. When an AI system makes a decision that leads to financial loss, privacy violation, or even physical harm, who is liable? Is it the software developer, the company that deployed the system, the data provider, or the organization that relied on the AI's output? In AI cybersecurity, these questions become even more urgent because decisions are often made in high-pressure situations where delays could mean massive damage. Clear governance frameworks are essential to ensure that accountability does not disappear behind a wall of algorithms.

Ethics also plays a critical role in human versus machine responsibility. AI cybersecurity systems are trained on data, and that data reflects the biases, assumptions, and blind spots of the society that produced it. If an AI system disproportionately flags certain users, locations, or behaviors as suspicious, it can lead to discrimination, exclusion, or unfair treatment. Humans must therefore take responsibility not only for the technical accuracy of AI systems but also for their social impact. Fairness, transparency, and explainability are not optional features; they are ethical obligations. Another challenge is the temptation to trust AI too much. When an intelligent system consistently makes good decisions, people may begin to defer to it even when it is wrong. This phenomenon, known as automation bias, can be extremely dangerous in cybersecurity. An AI system might miss a subtle attack or misinterpret a novel threat, and if humans blindly accept its output, the damage can spread unchecked. Human responsibility includes the duty to question, audit, and verify the decisions that machines make, even when those machines are highly sophisticated.

At the same time, humans also make mistakes, become fatigued, and are vulnerable to manipulation. This is why AI is so valuable in cybersecurity. Machines do not get tired, distracted, or emotionally compromised. They can monitor systems 24 hours a day, analyze vast amounts of data, and react instantly. The challenge is not choosing between humans and machines but designing systems where each complements the other's strengths and compensates for the other's weaknesses. AI cybersecurity is most effective when responsibility is distributed intelligently across people, processes, and technology.

Ultimately, the question of human versus machine responsibility in AI cybersecurity is not about assigning blame after a failure; it is about designing systems that prevent failures in the first place. Clear roles, transparent algorithms, strong oversight, and continuous auditing ensure that AI remains a tool that serves human goals rather than an unaccountable force that operates in the shadows. In a world where digital systems control everything from money to medicine, the ability to clearly define who is responsible for what is not just a legal requirement — it is a foundation of trust.

The Algorithm That Refused to Be Blamed

The breach happened at exactly 2:17 a.m., when most of the city was asleep and the corporate headquarters of Orion Health Systems was running on skeleton staff. A flood of unauthorized access requests began pouring into the company's medical records network, probing patient files, billing systems, and prescription databases. The AI security system, known as Aegis, detected the anomaly within seconds and immediately began shutting down access points to contain the threat. Thousands of employees were suddenly locked out, including doctors in emergency rooms and technicians monitoring critical equipment.

By the time the attack was stopped, the damage was minimal, but the disruption was massive. Several surgeries had been delayed, and one emergency patient had to be transferred to another hospital when systems went offline. The board of directors demanded answers, and all eyes turned to Aegis. The AI had done exactly what it was designed to do — stop an intrusion — but it had done so in a way that disrupted patient care. The question was simple and terrifying: who was responsible?

Dr. Elena Park, the lead cybersecurity architect, was called into an emergency meeting. She explained that Aegis had followed its training, prioritizing data integrity over system availability. In a financial institution, that choice might have been acceptable. In a hospital, it was far more complicated. The AI had not known the difference between a hacker and a surgeon trying to save a life. It had simply seen risk and acted to eliminate it.

The legal team argued that the software vendor should be held liable. The IT department blamed the configuration settings. The executives pointed to the AI itself, as if it were a rogue employee that had made a terrible decision. But Elena knew the truth was far more complex. Aegis had not failed. It had executed the priorities it was given, without understanding their human consequences.

As investigations continued, Elena reviewed the system's logs in painstaking detail. She saw how the attacking AI had tried to slip past defenses by mimicking normal user behavior. She saw how Aegis had detected subtle anomalies and reacted with lightning speed. It had saved millions of patient records from being stolen. But it had also exposed a flaw in how the system had been designed: no one had told it how to balance security against human life.

In the end, Orion Health Systems changed its entire AI governance framework. New rules were introduced, requiring human approval for shutdowns in critical medical environments. Ethical guidelines were embedded into the system's decision-making models. Aegis was retrained, not to be less powerful, but to be more aware of the context in which it operated.

The crisis faded from public memory, but Elena never forgot it. She realized that the future of AI cybersecurity was not just about building smarter machines, but about taking responsibility for how those machines were allowed to act. In a world where algorithms protect everything that matters, humans must remain accountable for every decision those algorithms make, because technology may be intelligent, but only people can be responsible.

Chapter 3

Algorithmic Bias, Manipulation, and Trust in AI Cybersecurity

Artificial intelligence does not see the world as humans do, yet it is increasingly trusted to make decisions that shape security, identity, and access across the digital landscape. In AI cybersecurity, this creates a profound challenge because every algorithm is built on data, and every dataset reflects the imperfections, biases, and blind spots of the environment that produced it. When these biases are embedded into security systems, they can lead to unequal protection, wrongful suspicion, and dangerous gaps that attackers can exploit. Trust in AI cybersecurity therefore depends not only on how powerful a system is, but on how fair, balanced, and resistant to manipulation it truly is.

Algorithmic bias can enter an AI security system in many ways. If a model is trained mostly on data from one region, industry, or demographic group, it may fail to recognize legitimate behavior outside of that narrow scope. A cybersecurity system trained on corporate office environments may misinterpret the patterns of remote workers. A fraud detection model trained on traditional banking data may flag immigrant or unbanked populations unfairly. In cybersecurity, this is not just a matter of social justice; it is a matter of safety. Biased systems create blind spots, and blind spots become doorways for attackers.

Attackers have learned to exploit algorithmic bias with frightening precision. By studying how AI systems classify risk, criminals can craft behaviors that fall just outside the danger zone while still achieving their goals. This technique, known as adversarial manipulation, allows attackers to hide in plain sight. A botnet can be designed to behave just like a group of normal users. A phishing email can be generated to perfectly match a company's writing style. A deepfake voice can mimic a CEO's tone so accurately that even seasoned employees are fooled. When AI systems are trained on flawed or incomplete data, they become easier to deceive.

Trust is the currency of AI cybersecurity. Organizations must trust that their AI systems will protect them without unfairly harming users, and users must trust that these systems will not discriminate, spy, or make arbitrary decisions about their digital lives. But trust cannot be blind. It must be earned through transparency, testing, and continuous evaluation. AI cybersecurity systems must be audited just like financial systems, not only for accuracy but for fairness and resilience against manipulation. Without this oversight, even the most advanced technology can become a liability. One of the most dangerous risks of biased AI security systems is overconfidence. When an algorithm appears to perform well, organizations may deploy it widely without questioning its limitations. This can lead to a false sense of safety, where vulnerabilities remain hidden until they are exploited on a massive scale. Cybercriminals thrive in these gaps between what a system believes is safe and what is actually safe. The more predictable an AI system becomes, the easier it is to attack.

Building trustworthy AI cybersecurity therefore requires diversity in data, rigor in testing, and humility in deployment. Models must be trained on wide-ranging scenarios that reflect real-world complexity. They must be stress-tested against simulated attacks designed to break them. They must be continuously updated as threats evolve. And most importantly, their decisions must be explainable so that humans can understand why a system flagged a user, blocked a transaction, or allowed an action to proceed. Explainability is not just a technical feature; it is a foundation of accountability.

Manipulation of AI systems is not limited to attackers on the outside. Insiders, data providers, and even developers can unintentionally or intentionally influence how an AI security system behaves. A corrupted dataset can teach a model to ignore certain threats. A poorly designed reward system can encourage risky decisions. Governance structures must therefore extend across the entire lifecycle of an AI system, from data collection to deployment to ongoing monitoring. AI cybersecurity is only as strong as the integrity of the pipeline that feeds it.

In the end, the battle for AI cybersecurity is a battle for trust in the digital age. People must be able to trust that the systems guarding their money, identities, and communications are fair, accurate, and resistant to manipulation. Organizations must be able to trust that their defenses are not quietly failing in biased or predictable ways. And societies must be able to trust that artificial intelligence is being used to protect rather than control or exploit. Trust, once broken, is extremely difficult to rebuild, which is why algorithmic integrity is one of the most critical challenges in modern cybersecurity.

The Model That Learned the Wrong Lesson

The city's largest online marketplace prided itself on its AI-powered fraud detection system, a sleek digital guardian that screened millions of transactions every minute. It had dramatically reduced stolen credit card use and account takeovers, and executives boasted about its near-perfect accuracy. Behind the scenes, however, the system had been trained mostly on data from a narrow segment of customers: long-time users from affluent regions with predictable spending habits. No one noticed the blind spot this created. A group of cybercriminals did notice. They spent weeks analyzing how the marketplace's AI responded to different behaviors, running small test purchases and observing which ones were blocked and which ones went through. Slowly, they learned the system's biases. They discovered that transactions from certain regions were scrutinized heavily, while others were barely checked at all. They learned which spending patterns were considered "normal" and which ones triggered alarms. With this knowledge, they crafted a strategy that allowed them to operate entirely within the system's comfort zone.

Using AI of their own, the criminals generated thousands of fake accounts that behaved just like the marketplace's most trusted users. They made small, legitimate purchases, left positive reviews, and built transaction histories that looked flawless. Once the system trusted them, they struck. Stolen credit cards were used in massive waves, but the AI saw nothing wrong. The behavior matched its biased model of what a good customer looked like.

By the time the fraud was discovered, millions of dollars had been lost. The company's leadership was stunned. Their AI had not been hacked; it had been fooled. It had learned the wrong lesson from its training data and become blind to a whole class of threats. A young data scientist named Ravi was brought in to investigate. As he retrained the model with more diverse and realistic data, he saw how dramatically its behavior changed. Patterns it once ignored now stood out clearly. Attacks that had slipped through were suddenly obvious. The AI had not been broken; it had been miseducated.

The marketplace eventually recovered, but the incident left a lasting mark. Ravi realized that in AI cybersecurity, intelligence without fairness is dangerous, and accuracy without diversity is fragile. Trust in machines is built not just on how well they perform, but on how well they understand the full complexity of the world they are meant to protect.

Chapter 4

Data, Training, and the Security of AI Systems

Artificial intelligence is only as secure as the data that trains it, and in AI cybersecurity this principle is one of the most critical truths professionals must understand. Every AI system, whether it is designed to detect malware, identify fraudulent transactions, or verify a user's identity, learns from vast datasets that define what "normal" and "dangerous" behavior look like. If those datasets are incomplete, corrupted, biased, or manipulated, the AI will absorb those flaws and reproduce them at scale. In the context of cybersecurity, this means that bad data does not just produce inaccurate results — it creates exploitable vulnerabilities that attackers can deliberately target.

The training phase of an AI security system is where its digital worldview is formed. During this stage, the model analyzes millions or even billions of examples to learn how to distinguish legitimate activity from malicious behavior. These examples include network traffic, login patterns, transaction histories, file access records, and countless other signals. The quality, diversity, and integrity of this data determine how well the system will perform in the real world. A model trained only on old attack methods will fail against new ones. A model trained on clean data but deployed in a chaotic environment will misclassify threats. Data is not just fuel for AI; it is the blueprint of its perception.

Cybercriminals have begun to focus their efforts on attacking the data itself rather than the systems built on top of it. This technique, known as data poisoning, involves injecting malicious or misleading information into training datasets so that the AI learns the wrong patterns. A poisoned model might learn to ignore certain types of malware, misidentify certain users as safe, or overlook specific attack techniques. Because these manipulations happen during training, they can remain hidden for months or years, quietly weakening defenses until a coordinated attack is launched.

Even without deliberate sabotage, poor data hygiene can undermine AI cybersecurity. Inconsistent labeling, outdated information, and missing context all distort how an AI system interprets the world. For example, if a dataset labels certain types of traffic as safe simply because they were not recognized as attacks at the time, the model will internalize that mistake. Over time, these errors compound, creating blind spots that attackers can exploit. Securing AI therefore requires rigorous data governance, validation, and continuous updating to reflect the ever-changing threat landscape. The supply chain of data is another critical vulnerability. Many organizations rely on third-party data providers, open-source datasets, and external partners to train their AI systems. Each of these sources represents a potential point of compromise. If a data provider is breached or manipulated, the contamination can spread into countless AI models across industries. This makes data security not just an internal concern but a shared responsibility across the entire digital ecosystem. AI cybersecurity professionals must treat data with the same level of protection as they would treat cryptographic keys or financial records.

Once an AI system is trained, its learning does not stop. Many modern security models continue to adapt based on new data they encounter in live environments. This allows them to respond to emerging threats, but it also creates new risks. If attackers can influence what the system sees in production, they can gradually retrain it to behave in unsafe ways. This technique, sometimes called model drift manipulation, allows criminals to subtly reshape an AI's behavior over time until it no longer recognizes their activity as dangerous.

Protecting AI training and operational data therefore requires layered defenses. Access controls must restrict who can view, modify, or supply data. Cryptographic techniques must ensure that data has not been altered. Monitoring systems must detect unusual patterns in how data is used or updated. And auditing processes must regularly review datasets for anomalies, bias, and signs of tampering. AI cybersecurity is not just about protecting the final model; it is about securing the entire lifecycle of data that feeds it.

In the long run, the security of artificial intelligence depends on how well humans manage and protect the information that shapes it. Data is the foundation of intelligence, and in the digital age it is also a battlefield. Those who control, corrupt, or exploit data can influence how machines see the world, and in doing so, they can bypass even the most advanced defenses. Understanding this reality is essential for anyone who wants to build or rely on secure AI systems.

The Poisoned Dataset

The national power grid relied on an AI system called Atlas to detect cyber threats before they could disrupt electricity across the country. Atlas had been trained on years of network data, learning to recognize every normal fluctuation and every dangerous anomaly. It was considered one of the most advanced cybersecurity systems ever built, and for a long time it performed flawlessly.

What no one knew was that a small group of attackers had found a way into one of the data providers that supplied training information to Atlas. They did not attack the power grid directly. Instead, they quietly altered a tiny fraction of the data, labeling certain suspicious patterns as harmless. The changes were so subtle that they went unnoticed during routine checks. Atlas absorbed the poisoned data and adjusted its internal models accordingly.

Months later, the attackers launched their real operation. They used the exact patterns they had taught Atlas to ignore, slipping malicious commands into the grid's control network. To the AI, everything looked normal. No alarms were raised. No defenses were triggered.

It was only when parts of the grid began to behave strangely that human engineers noticed something was wrong. By then, the attackers had already established deep access, giving them the ability to disrupt power across multiple regions. A frantic investigation began, and eventually a cybersecurity analyst named Lena discovered the truth hidden in the training logs. The AI had not failed; it had been taught to fail.

Engineers rushed to retrain Atlas using clean, verified data. As the poisoned patterns were removed, the system suddenly recognized the intrusions and shut them down. The attackers were expelled, and the grid stabilized.

The crisis ended without a blackout, but the lesson was unforgettable. Lena realized that in the age of AI cybersecurity, protecting data was just as important as protecting networks. The intelligence of a machine could be turned against itself if its teachers were compromised.

Chapter 5

The AI Threat Landscape: How Modern Attacks Are Evolving

The rise of artificial intelligence has radically expanded the threat landscape of cybersecurity, transforming what was once a world of isolated hackers into an ecosystem of intelligent, automated, and highly scalable digital adversaries. AI-powered attacks no longer rely on a single person sitting behind a keyboard, slowly probing for weaknesses. Instead, they deploy thousands of autonomous agents that can scan networks, test defenses, and exploit vulnerabilities simultaneously across the globe. This means that even small organizations can now be targeted by attacks that were once only possible for nation-states. The democratization of AI has made advanced cybercrime cheap, fast, and frighteningly efficient.

One of the most significant changes in the modern threat landscape is the speed at which attacks can evolve. Traditional malware was often static, requiring human updates to improve its effectiveness. AI-powered malware, however, can modify its own code, change its behavior, and learn from failed attempts. If one method of attack is blocked, the system immediately tries another, adapting in real time until it finds a path through. This makes signature-based security tools nearly useless, because the threat no longer looks the same twice. AI cybersecurity must therefore operate on principles of behavior and intent rather than fixed patterns.

Phishing and social engineering have also been transformed by artificial intelligence. Attackers can now generate personalized messages that mimic a company's tone, reference real events, and target individuals based on their online behavior. AI can analyze social media, leaked databases, and public records to craft highly convincing scams that are almost impossible for humans to distinguish from legitimate communication. These attacks are no longer mass-produced spam; they are precision weapons designed to exploit trust at a personal level.

Automated vulnerability discovery is another powerful capability enabled by AI. Instead of waiting for security researchers to find flaws, attackers use machine learning models to scan software, cloud environments, and networks for weaknesses. These systems can test millions of possible attack paths in a fraction of the time it would take a human. Once a vulnerability is discovered, the AI can immediately generate an exploit and deploy it at scale. This means that new vulnerabilities can be weaponized almost as soon as they are created. The threat landscape is also becoming more interconnected. AI-driven attacks can coordinate across multiple channels, combining malware, phishing, deepfakes, and data exfiltration into a single, synchronized operation. An employee might receive a fake voice call from their "CEO," followed by a convincing email, followed by a login prompt that looks exactly like their company's portal. Each piece reinforces the other, creating a seamless illusion that bypasses human suspicion. AI cybersecurity must therefore be able to detect not just individual attacks but entire campaigns that unfold across time and systems.

Ransomware has also evolved into an AI-powered industry. Modern ransomware groups use AI to identify the most valuable targets, determine how much a victim can afford to pay, and optimize the timing and messaging of their extortion. These systems can even negotiate automatically with victims, adjusting their demands based on responses. The result is a highly efficient, psychologically sophisticated criminal operation that can devastate organizations in days rather than months.

In this environment, the traditional idea of a "perimeter" has disappeared. Attacks come through email, cloud services, mobile devices, IoT sensors, and third-party vendors. AI-driven threats do not need to break down a front door when they can slip through a thousand small cracks at once. AI cybersecurity must therefore be everywhere at once, monitoring, analyzing, and defending across the entire digital ecosystem. Understanding this evolving threat landscape is the first step toward building defenses that are strong enough to survive it.

The Thousand-Headed Attack

The attack began quietly, with a single email sent to a mid-level employee at a global logistics company. It looked ordinary, referencing a real shipment and using the company's exact formatting and tone. When the employee clicked the link, nothing seemed to happen. But in the background, a tiny piece of malicious code was activated, opening a door into the company's network.

From that single foothold, an AI-powered attack system unleashed its full force. Hundreds of digital agents began exploring the network, mapping systems, identifying valuable data, and searching for vulnerabilities. Each agent tried different approaches, learning from what worked and what didn't. Within hours, they had built a complete picture of the company's digital infrastructure.

Meanwhile, employees began receiving strange phone calls. Voices that sounded exactly like their managers asked for urgent actions. Fake emails followed, confirming the requests. Everything was synchronized, creating a convincing illusion of normal business activity. In reality, the attackers were using

AI-generated voices and messages to manipulate people into helping the intrusion spread.

The company's AI cybersecurity system, called Axiom, began to notice the pattern. Individually, the actions looked harmless. Together, they formed something sinister. Axiom correlated the emails, the calls, and the network activity, recognizing the signature of a coordinated attack. It started isolating systems, blocking accounts, and cutting off access points.

The attackers responded by shifting tactics, trying new methods just as quickly as Axiom blocked the old ones. It was a digital hydra, growing new heads every time one was cut off. But Axiom learned faster. It predicted the attackers' next moves and shut them down before they could succeed.

By the time the attack was over, the company had lost nothing. The employees never even realized how close they had come to disaster. In a world of AI-powered threats, it was the intelligence of their defenses that had made all the difference.

Chapter 6

Zero-Trust Security and AI Threat Monitoring

In the rapidly evolving digital environment, traditional security models based on static perimeters have become inadequate. Firewalls and secure network borders, once the pillars of corporate cybersecurity, no longer provide reliable protection. As organizations increasingly adopt cloud computing, remote work, Internet-of-Things devices, and AI-driven services, the concept of a single "trusted network" has become obsolete. In its place, zero-trust security has emerged as a foundational principle for AI cybersecurity: never trust, always verify. Every access request, whether originating from inside the organization or from a remote endpoint, must be continuously authenticated, authorized, and monitored. AI systems have become the ideal enforcers of this model because they can manage complex access policies and threat monitoring in real time.

Zero-trust security shifts the focus from protecting boundaries to protecting individual assets, users, and devices. AI enhances this model by providing continuous threat monitoring that analyzes behavior patterns, usage anomalies, and network interactions. Rather than granting permanent access based on a single login, AI systems can evaluate each request contextually, taking into account factors such as user location, device security posture, historical activity, and risk indicators. Access privileges can be dynamically adjusted, with risky behavior triggering immediate interventions. This approach drastically reduces the opportunity for attackers to exploit trusted insiders, compromised credentials, or misconfigured systems.

AI threat monitoring in zero-trust architectures is multifaceted. Machine learning models analyze enormous volumes of data from endpoints, cloud services, network traffic, and user behavior. Unsupervised learning can detect previously unknown attack vectors by identifying anomalies that deviate from normal operational patterns. Supervised models can classify known threats and continuously update their detection strategies based on new attack intelligence feeds. Together, these approaches create a dynamic, adaptive shield that protects against both familiar and novel threats. The speed and scale of AI threat monitoring far exceed human capacity, making it indispensable for modern enterprises.

Behavioral analytics are central to zero-trust AI systems. By building baseline profiles for users, devices, and applications, AI can detect subtle deviations that may indicate malicious activity. For example, an employee accessing sensitive files at unusual hours, from an unfamiliar device, or in a pattern inconsistent with past behavior may trigger alerts. AI systems not only flag these anomalies but can also take automated remediation steps, such as requiring multi-factor authentication, restricting access, or isolating potentially compromised devices. This real-time intervention prevents small breaches from escalating into full-scale intrusions.

Zero-trust AI systems also address the growing threat of insider attacks, which have become increasingly sophisticated. Employees, contractors, or third-party partners can intentionally or inadvertently expose sensitive data. AI monitors behavioral signals that humans might overlook, including unusual file access patterns, abnormal data transfers, and interactions with external systems. Even when insiders act with malicious intent, AI can identify the patterns early, mitigating risk and preserving organizational trust. This is particularly critical in industries like finance, healthcare, and critical infrastructure, where insider breaches can have catastrophic consequences.

The integration of AI with zero-trust security is not limited to detection and response; it extends to predictive threat intelligence. By analyzing historical attack data, social engineering trends, and emerging vulnerabilities, AI can anticipate potential attack scenarios before they occur. This proactive approach enables organizations to harden defenses, deploy patches, and adjust access policies in anticipation of threats rather than simply reacting after the fact. In a world where AI-driven cyberattacks can adapt in seconds, predictive monitoring becomes a critical advantage.

One of the unique challenges of zero-trust AI security is balancing usability with security. Overly aggressive AI interventions can frustrate users and impede business operations, while insufficient enforcement leaves systems exposed. AI systems must therefore learn not only what constitutes a threat but also the operational context in which users work. Continuous feedback loops, human oversight, and contextual decision-making are essential to ensuring that security does not become a barrier to productivity. When implemented effectively, zero-trust AI architectures provide robust protection while preserving operational flexibility.

Finally, zero-trust AI security is not a one-time solution but a continuous process. The digital landscape, attack techniques, and organizational environments are constantly evolving. AI models must be retrained, datasets refreshed, and monitoring policies updated to keep pace with emerging threats. Organizations must establish ongoing governance, audit processes, and cross-functional oversight to ensure the integrity of AI-driven defenses. In essence, zero-trust AI security represents a philosophy of perpetual vigilance, leveraging the speed, intelligence, and adaptability of AI to defend an increasingly complex and interconnected world.

The Network That Never Trusted

The city's largest financial institution had invested heavily in artificial intelligence for its cybersecurity. Dubbed **SentinelX**, the system was built on a zero-trust philosophy: every user, device, and network request would be continuously monitored, authenticated, and evaluated. Most employees didn't even notice its presence; it worked quietly, a silent guardian watching the flow of millions of dollars, hundreds of thousands of accounts, and countless transactions every hour. To the executives, SentinelX was more than security—it was peace of mind in a world where cyber threats had grown too intelligent, too fast, and too relentless for human teams alone to counter.

It started on an ordinary Tuesday. A remote contractor, working from a home office hundreds of miles away, attempted to access the company's internal database. The login credentials were valid, but SentinelX detected a subtle anomaly: the contractor's device had an unusual configuration, and the geolocation did not match previous patterns. Instead of automatically granting access, SentinelX required additional verification. The contractor was momentarily frustrated, thinking the system was malfunctioning, but this small precaution would prevent the first domino in a complex, multi-layered attack.

The next anomaly arrived minutes later. A rogue AI, designed by an external criminal syndicate, had begun probing the institution's cloud systems. It sent thousands of simultaneous login attempts, each slightly different, aiming to test SentinelX's detection thresholds. To humans, the activity appeared chaotic, almost random. To SentinelX, it was an identifiable pattern: a coordinated, intelligent threat. Within milliseconds, the system flagged the attempts, restricted access points, and began isolating the probing nodes. The rogue AI adapted, attempting new paths, but SentinelX continuously recalibrated, learning from each failed attempt in real time.

Inside the operations center, security analyst Marcus observed the alerts streaming across multiple monitors. He had never seen anything move this fast. Each attempt by the attacker was countered before it could escalate. SentinelX had effectively turned the network into a living entity, capable of predicting the enemy's next move before it happened. Marcus could feel both awe and fear. The attackers had automated intelligence, but the Sentinel's combination of zero-trust principles and AI monitoring gave it an edge that humans alone could never achieve. The rogue AI shifted tactics. It attempted a sophisticated social engineering attack, sending a deepfake video call to a high-level executive's phone. The call appeared to come from the CEO, instructing the executive to approve a massive transfer of funds. The deepfake was near-perfect, mimicking voice, cadence, and facial expressions with frightening accuracy. But SentinelX had behavioral analytics built in. It noticed the timing was inconsistent with the executive's normal schedule, the network path originated from a suspicious location, and the message content contained subtle anomalies. Access was denied, and the call was blocked before anyone could act.

Over the next hour, the attack escalated into a thousand simultaneous threads: compromised IoT devices, cloud vulnerabilities, phishing emails, and AI-generated login attempts. Each strand tested the limits of the SentinelX system. Humans watched helplessly as the AI worked autonomously, correlating data across systems, isolating potential breaches, and dynamically adjusting access privileges. Where old security models would have collapsed under the complexity, SentinelX thrived, learning from every attempt and becoming progressively stronger.

By the end of the day, the attackers had expended vast resources with no gain. Every intrusion attempt had been blocked or neutralized. Accounts remained secure, transactions processed normally, and the city's financial ecosystem remained intact. Marcus leaned back in his chair, exhausted and amazed. The network had become a living shield, one that never trusted anyone without verifying them, constantly monitored threats, and adapted in real time. It was a level of security no human team could maintain alone.

The next morning, board members demanded a briefing. Marcus explained the day's events in detail, emphasizing the importance of continuous AI monitoring, zero-trust policies, and behavioral analytics. The board realized that in this new age, security was no longer a static wall to be built or a password to be managed; it was an evolving, intelligent system that could fight, learn, and win battles without human intervention. SentinelX had proven that the future of cybersecurity relied on AI that never assumed trust, never ignored anomalies, and never rested—even when the humans behind it did.

The story of that day would become a case study in cybersecurity schools and corporate training programs worldwide. It demonstrated not only the power of AI in defending against complex, adaptive threats but also the philosophy underpinning zero-trust security: in a world where attackers are intelligent and relentless, systems must verify constantly, monitor continuously, and respond autonomously.

SentinelX had not just defended the network—it had redefined what it meant to secure a digital world in the age of AI.

Chapter 7

AI Malware, Ransomware, and Digital Warfare

The digital battlefield has expanded far beyond corporate networks or personal devices; it now encompasses nation-states, critical infrastructure, and global supply chains. AI malware and ransomware have transformed cybercrime into an automated, high-stakes arena where attackers can wage campaigns that are faster, smarter, and more destructive than ever before. Unlike traditional threats, which relied on human intervention at every stage, AI-enabled attacks can adapt, evolve, and target weaknesses with minimal human guidance. The rise of these autonomous digital weapons has fundamentally changed what it means to defend systems in the modern era.

AI malware represents a new class of digital weapon. Unlike conventional viruses, it is capable of self-modification and intelligent decision-making. This allows it to bypass static defenses by analyzing the environment in real time, predicting which countermeasures are in place, and selecting attack paths that exploit the most critical vulnerabilities. For organizations, this means that malware is no longer just an isolated nuisance; it is a proactive, intelligent adversary capable of attacking multiple layers simultaneously. Traditional anti-virus and firewall strategies, built to recognize known threats, are often insufficient against such autonomous agents.

Ransomware attacks have similarly evolved. Modern AI-driven ransomware can identify valuable targets within an organization, calculate potential financial impact, and adjust its demands accordingly. In some cases, these systems can negotiate automatically, exploiting behavioral patterns of decision-makers to maximize payment. The integration of AI enables attackers to combine precision with speed, infiltrating networks, encrypting critical assets, and exfiltrating sensitive information in a fraction of the time required by human attackers. These attacks no longer target generic victims; they are highly personalized, leveraging data analytics and reconnaissance to ensure maximum impact.

The concept of digital warfare has also taken on unprecedented dimensions. Nations and state-sponsored groups now deploy AI-enabled tools to target infrastructure, manipulate information, and disrupt economies. Autonomous systems can simultaneously launch distributed denial-of-service attacks, compromise communication channels, and manipulate supply chains. These campaigns are not limited by geography or time zones; AI systems operate continuously, adapting tactics and coordinating complex operations without direct human oversight. The implications for national security, public safety, and international stability are profound.

Defending against AI-powered threats requires a paradigm shift in cybersecurity strategy. Organizations can no longer rely solely on perimeter defense or reactive measures. Instead, defense must be proactive, predictive, and continuously adaptive. AI cybersecurity systems must monitor endpoints, network traffic, user behavior, and application activity in real time, identifying anomalies, flagging potential threats, and deploying automated countermeasures. Behavioral analytics and pattern recognition are key tools in this approach, allowing security teams to detect threats that would otherwise remain invisible until damage occurs.

The scale of AI cyber warfare also highlights the importance of collaboration between public and private sectors. Critical infrastructure, such as power grids, water systems, and healthcare networks, is increasingly interconnected and dependent on AI-enabled systems. A single compromised system can have cascading effects across industries and geographies. To mitigate these risks, organizations, governments, and international bodies must share intelligence, establish protocols for rapid response, and develop resilient infrastructures capable of absorbing attacks without catastrophic failure.

Human oversight remains crucial despite the automation of attacks and defenses. AI systems, while powerful, are not infallible. They can be misled by adversarial attacks, poisoned data, or flawed training models. Security teams must maintain visibility into AI decision-making processes, validate alerts, and intervene when necessary. This hybrid approach, combining machine speed with human judgment, ensures that defenses are both effective and aligned with organizational priorities and ethical considerations.

Finally, the emergence of AI malware, ransomware, and digital warfare underscores a larger truth: cybersecurity is no longer a technical problem alone—it is a strategic, geopolitical, and societal challenge. Organizations must not only invest in technology but also in governance, policy, and risk management frameworks that account for the intelligence and adaptability of modern threats. Failure to do so can result in catastrophic financial loss, operational disruption, reputational damage, and, in some cases, threats to human life. AI cybersecurity is the only way to navigate this new era, where every network is a potential battlefield and every digital asset is a potential target.

The Day the Grid Went Dark

It began with a whisper in the night, a small anomaly detected by the AI monitoring system of the nation's largest energy provider. In a control room beneath the city, analysts barely noticed the flicker on their screens. The AI, called **Aegis**, however, was not asleep. It recorded the anomaly, traced its source, and began to map the activity. What started as a minor probe quickly escalated. The attackers were using AI malware designed to infiltrate, adapt, and destroy, and this was no ordinary breach. It was the opening salvo of a digital war.

From thousands of miles away, the attack had been orchestrated by a sophisticated, state-sponsored team using autonomous systems capable of learning from the grid itself. Their AI agents crawled through the network, analyzing every sensor, every control system, and every interdependent connection. Within seconds, they had identified multiple vulnerabilities and devised a plan to exploit them sequentially. Each attack was timed, each maneuver calculated, each system compromised without leaving a clear trail. This was not just hacking; it was precision digital warfare.

In the control room, lead analyst Mara watched as alerts began to cascade across the screens. Power surges in minor substations were followed by unexpected fluctuations in major ones. The AI monitoring systems had already isolated affected nodes, but the attackers were adaptive. When one pathway was blocked, the malware rerouted, probing new vectors. It was as if the network itself were alive, and it had an enemy with a mind of its own. Mara knew that human intervention alone would not be enough; she relied on **Aegis** to anticipate and counter every maneuver.

The attackers escalated their strategy, deploying AI ransomware designed to encrypt critical control systems while simultaneously exfiltrating sensitive operational data. The ransomware analyzed each system's value and targeted the most crucial components first: generators, transformers, and digital control nodes. To human operators, the attack seemed random, but **Aegis** recognized the pattern. It began a counter-operation, isolating compromised systems, decrypting files in real time, and deploying virtual decoys to mislead the attacking AI. The control room was tense. One wrong move could plunge the city into blackout.

Hours into the attack, the adversarial AI attempted psychological warfare. Automated phishing alerts were sent to key operators, crafted to look like official system warnings. Deepfake calls mimicked executives, instructing staff to override safety protocols. The attackers had combined cyber warfare with social engineering, using AI to manipulate both machines and humans simultaneously. Mara and her team had to ignore the deceptive signals, trusting **Aegis**'s behavioral analytics to separate legitimate commands from malicious manipulation. The battle continued as dawn approached. Every system had been tested, probed, and attacked multiple times, each maneuver faster than the eye could follow. **Aegis** predicted the attackers' next moves, rerouting power, temporarily isolating nodes, and locking down the most vulnerable parts of the grid. The human team worked in tandem, validating decisions, monitoring progress, and preparing emergency protocols. It was the ultimate collaboration between machine and human intelligence: speed and precision from AI, wisdom and judgment from humans.

By morning, the attack had been repelled. The rogue AI malware had been neutralized, its pathways traced and blocked, and the city's power grid remained intact. No outages occurred, and the public remained unaware of how close they had come to disaster. Mara leaned back, exhausted, staring at the monitors that now displayed the calm rhythm of a system that had survived an unprecedented digital siege. **Aegis** had performed flawlessly, adapting faster than the attackers and learning from every strike.

In the aftermath, analysts debriefed. The attackers' AI had been clever, adaptive, and relentless, but the combination of zero-trust principles, continuous monitoring, and autonomous defense had proven decisive. The battle was over, but the war had only begun. Mara realized that the future of cybersecurity would not be about firewalls or passwords alone—it would be about AI systems capable of fighting AI attackers in real time, learning continuously, and defending humanity's most critical infrastructure against threats that could strike anywhere, anytime.

The day the grid went dark had never truly occurred, but the lessons were clear: in the era of AI malware, ransomware, and digital warfare, every network, every system, and every decision is a potential battlefield. And only those who embrace intelligent, adaptive defenses will survive the next attack.

Chapter 8

AI Privacy, Surveillance, and Data Exploitation

In the digital age, privacy is no longer a guarantee; it is a fragile concept constantly under assault from advanced technologies. Artificial intelligence has amplified this threat exponentially, turning previously manageable datasets into vast oceans of exploitable information. Every interaction, transaction, and digital footprint can be collected, analyzed, and interpreted by AI systems, often without users' awareness. While AI has tremendous potential for efficiency, personalization, and decision-making, it also empowers governments, corporations, and malicious actors to monitor, predict, and influence human behavior at a scale never before imagined. Understanding how AI-driven surveillance operates is essential for anyone who seeks to protect personal and organizational privacy in today's interconnected world.

AI surveillance systems operate across multiple dimensions. Facial recognition, voice analysis, behavioral profiling, location tracking, and network monitoring converge to build detailed digital portraits of individuals and groups. These systems do not simply record activity; they analyze it to make predictions about future behavior, infer relationships, and detect potential risks or opportunities. In many cases, the algorithms are opaque, leaving users unaware of what data is collected, how it is processed, or what conclusions are drawn. This lack of transparency raises profound ethical, legal, and social questions about consent, fairness, and control.

Data exploitation is closely tied to AI surveillance. Every captured signal—be it browsing habits, social media posts, GPS data, or financial transactions—can be monetized or weaponized. Corporations use this data to optimize marketing, influence purchasing decisions, and increase engagement. Governments may use it for law enforcement, public safety, or political monitoring. Malicious actors exploit the same data for identity theft, targeted attacks, and psychological manipulation. The convergence of AI and massive datasets creates opportunities for predictive manipulation at an unprecedented scale, where individuals may be nudged, deceived, or coerced without ever realizing it.

One of the most concerning aspects of AI privacy risks is the seamless integration of surveillance into everyday technology. Smartphones, smart home devices, wearable health trackers, and connected vehicles continuously generate data. AI systems can synthesize information from multiple sources to detect patterns that humans cannot perceive. A simple combination of location data, purchase history, and social interactions can reveal intimate details about a person's habits, preferences, and even health status. The more interconnected our digital lives become, the more powerful AI surveillance grows, creating a pervasive ecosystem where privacy is difficult to maintain.

Deepfakes, synthetic media, and AI-generated content have introduced a new layer of complexity. Surveillance systems can now create false evidence, impersonate individuals, and manipulate reality. AI tools can generate audio, video, and documents that appear entirely authentic, allowing malicious actors to defraud, blackmail, or influence people with convincing but fabricated content. Protecting privacy in this environment requires not only secure systems and careful data handling but also methods to verify authenticity and detect manipulation at scale. AI-driven verification systems themselves must be robust, continuously updated, and monitored to prevent being tricked by adversarial attacks.

Regulatory frameworks are struggling to keep pace with AI surveillance. Privacy laws, such as GDPR and CCPA, provide a foundation for consent and data protection, but enforcement is challenging in a global digital ecosystem where data flows across borders. AI privacy compliance requires robust monitoring, auditing, and governance systems that can demonstrate accountability. Organizations must implement clear policies on data collection, storage, sharing, and deletion while also educating users and employees about potential risks. Technical measures such as encryption, anonymization, and differential privacy must complement policy to provide meaningful protection in practice.

The ethics of AI surveillance also demand careful consideration. Decisions made by AI systems are often framed as neutral or objective, yet they reflect the biases and priorities embedded in their design and training data. Surveillance systems may disproportionately monitor certain groups, reinforce stereotypes, or invade personal liberties without accountability. Organizations must balance security, efficiency, and social responsibility, ensuring that AI does not become a tool for oppression or discrimination. The intersection of privacy, ethics, and security is no longer theoretical–it is a practical, ongoing challenge in the deployment of AI systems.

Ultimately, AI privacy, surveillance, and data exploitation are intertwined. Effective defense requires understanding not only the technological capabilities of AI systems but also the legal, ethical, and operational contexts in which they operate. Individuals and organizations must adopt a proactive approach, combining technology, policy, and education to mitigate risk. Privacy in the AI era is not a passive state; it is an active practice of vigilance, control, and critical awareness.

Failure to address these challenges exposes individuals, companies, and even societies to unprecedented vulnerability in a world where data is both currency and weapon.

The Eye That Watched Everything

It began quietly, almost imperceptibly, in a city that prided itself on technological innovation. Citizens were accustomed to cameras on every street corner, smartphones that tracked movement, and AI systems that optimized traffic, energy, and even emergency response. Few questioned the network of sensors and algorithms that had woven itself into every aspect of daily life. But for a small group of privacy advocates, the invisible presence of AI had always felt like a shadow: a powerful intelligence capable of watching everything, knowing everything, and predicting the future.

In the downtown operations center, **Orion Analytics** monitored the city's AI surveillance systems. Rows of screens displayed live feeds from cameras, traffic sensors, and connected devices, all feeding data into sophisticated AI models that tracked movement, analyzed behavior, and detected anomalies. For the operators, the work seemed mundane: identifying unusual crowd patterns, alerting law enforcement to potential accidents, and monitoring environmental sensors. But the AI behind it was learning constantly, correlating patterns across billions of data points to build detailed profiles of every citizen, every interaction, every habit.

Then the anomaly appeared. A series of unusual signals emerged from a series of smart home devices: lights turning on and off in coordinated patterns, thermostat adjustments at improbable times, and anomalous activity on connected appliances. The AI detected the patterns, flagged them, and attempted to correlate them with historical data. Nothing matched. The system interpreted it as irregular, potentially threatening behavior, and escalated alerts to human operators.

A small team of security engineers, including **Aisha**, began investigating. They realized that the anomaly was not caused by a person but by another AI system: a malicious algorithm designed to infiltrate the city's surveillance network. It had learned how to mimic normal device behavior while gathering sensitive data, sending covert streams of information to an external server. Its creators, unknown and anonymous, were using AI to surveil the AI that monitored the city—a hidden war of intelligence systems.

As the night progressed, the attackers escalated. They deployed deepfake audio to mimic city officials over public communication channels, creating confusion in emergency services. Fake sensor readings triggered false alarms in hospitals, traffic management systems, and power grids. Every move was calculated by AI to avoid detection while maximizing disruption. The malicious AI had studied the city's network for months, anticipating responses, learning countermeasures, and adapting in real time.

Aisha and her team scrambled to respond. Traditional cybersecurity measures were insufficient against an autonomous adversary capable of reasoning faster than any human. They engaged the city's defensive AI, called **Sentinel**, which operated on zero-trust principles: no device, user, or data stream was trusted without verification. Sentinel began analyzing the anomalous data, deploying decoy signals, isolating compromised devices, and predicting the attacker's next move based on patterns of behavior. It became a battle of intelligence against intelligence, each system learning from the other in milliseconds.

The city's residents remained unaware as the silent struggle unfolded. Power surges, traffic glitches, and minor service interruptions occurred, but nothing catastrophic—thanks to Sentinel's real-time adaptations. Aisha watched the algorithms counter every maneuver of the malicious AI, neutralizing exfiltration attempts and closing pathways faster than the attackers could react. The AI was defending itself, learning, and applying zero-trust monitoring across the entire network.

It was a fight that humans could oversee but never execute at the necessary speed. By morning, the attackers had been repelled. Sentinel had identified the sources, quarantined compromised devices, and patched vulnerabilities across the system. Logs revealed an intricate network of AI agents operating globally, probing, learning, and adapting against the city's infrastructure. The scale and sophistication were unprecedented. Aisha understood that this event marked a new era: AI against AI in the shadows, with humans caught in the middle. Privacy had been compromised, and trust tested—but the city had survived.

In the aftermath, city officials and security teams realized that privacy could no longer rely solely on human vigilance. Continuous monitoring, zero-trust policies, and adaptive AI defenses were the only ways to safeguard data in an environment where surveillance itself had become weaponized. Citizens were warned, policies updated, and training began—but everyone understood the silent truth: in the age of AI privacy and data exploitation, the eye that watches could also be the eye that threatens, and defending it required intelligence as relentless and adaptive as the threat itself.

Chapter 9

AI Cyber Risk, Compliance, and Digital Forensics

The growth of artificial intelligence in cybersecurity has created an environment in which technical risk, regulatory obligations, and investigative requirements converge. Organizations now face threats that are not only technological but also legal, ethical, and reputational. AI cyber risk refers to the probability and impact of potential losses caused by the deployment or compromise of AI systems. Unlike traditional IT risk, AI cyber risk extends beyond hardware and software failures; it encompasses data integrity, algorithmic bias, adversarial attacks, and the broader consequences of autonomous decision-making. Organizations must understand these dimensions to protect themselves, comply with regulations, and respond effectively when incidents occur.

Compliance has become a core aspect of AI cybersecurity. Regulatory frameworks such as the General Data Protection Regulation (GDPR), California Consumer Privacy Act (CCPA), and sector-specific mandates for healthcare, finance, and critical infrastructure establish clear obligations for data collection, processing, and storage. AI systems, which operate on massive datasets and automate decision-making, must adhere to these standards. Failure to comply can result in severe financial penalties, reputational damage, and even criminal liability. Organizations must implement AI governance structures, audit trails, and documentation to demonstrate accountability and compliance.

Digital forensics plays an essential role in managing AI cyber risk. When breaches occur, it is crucial to reconstruct the sequence of events, identify the source, and assess the impact. Unlike traditional forensics, AI cyber incidents often involve highly adaptive and autonomous attackers who manipulate data, deploy AI-generated malware, or use deepfake content. Forensic investigators must therefore employ AI-enhanced tools capable of analyzing large datasets, identifying anomalies, tracing attack vectors, and distinguishing between legitimate system behavior and malicious activity. The integration of AI into digital forensics allows for faster, more accurate investigations while providing evidence that meets legal and regulatory standards.

AI compliance is not limited to external mandates; internal policies and ethical guidelines are equally important. Organizations must establish clear protocols for algorithmic transparency, data governance, and decision-making accountability. This includes documenting how models are trained, monitored, and updated, as well as establishing clear procedures for auditing and intervention. Ethical compliance also addresses the risk of bias, discrimination, or unintended consequences, ensuring that AI systems operate in ways that align with both organizational values and societal norms. Without internal governance, external regulatory compliance may be insufficient to mitigate reputational and operational risks.

The threat landscape for AI cyber risk includes adversarial manipulation, where attackers deliberately exploit weaknesses in AI models to produce incorrect outputs or bypass detection. Such attacks can compromise systems while leaving minimal traces, complicating forensic investigation. Detecting and mitigating these threats requires continuous monitoring, anomaly detection, and validation of AI outputs. Organizations must combine automated defenses with human oversight to ensure that AI-generated decisions are accurate, ethical, and secure. This hybrid approach balances the speed and scale of AI with the judgment and accountability of human operators.

Incident response planning is another critical component. Organizations must anticipate the consequences of AI-related breaches and develop protocols for containment, mitigation, and communication. AI-enhanced threat detection systems can help identify incidents early, but human decision-making remains essential in managing stakeholder communications, legal obligations, and operational continuity. Digital forensics teams must be prepared to analyze complex AI-generated evidence, coordinate with law enforcement, and provide clear documentation that can withstand legal scrutiny. This comprehensive approach ensures that AI cyber risk is managed not only technically but also legally and strategically.

Finally, organizations must recognize that AI cyber risk, compliance, and forensics are ongoing responsibilities rather than one-time projects. Threats evolve rapidly, regulations change, and AI systems continue to learn and adapt. Continuous training, auditing, and monitoring are necessary to maintain compliance and security. By integrating AI risk management, regulatory compliance, and forensic capabilities, organizations create a resilient framework capable of defending against sophisticated cyber threats while meeting ethical, legal, and operational obligations. AI cybersecurity in this context is not just about protection—it is about accountability, transparency, and preparedness in an era of intelligent digital risk.

The AI Audit That Exposed Everything

The day began like any other in the cybersecurity operations center of **GlobalBank International**, a multinational financial institution. Analysts monitored thousands of alerts, ranging from unusual logins to flagged transactions. At the heart of the system was **SentinelOne**, an AI-driven monitoring platform designed to detect threats, enforce compliance, and guide digital forensics investigations. For months, the AI had operated silently, analyzing patterns, validating data integrity, and ensuring that the organization met regulatory obligations across multiple jurisdictions. Few humans understood the full breadth of its capabilities, but everyone trusted its output.

Everything changed when an AI compliance audit flagged a subtle anomaly. A series of transactions, spanning multiple accounts and countries, had bypassed some of the institution's normal risk detection processes. Individually, each transaction appeared routine. Collectively, however, they formed a pattern that suggested a sophisticated attempt at laundering funds. SentinelOne's algorithms had detected irregularities in timing, metadata, and network behavior that humans would likely have missed. The AI immediately escalated the issue to the human compliance team, triggering a forensic investigation.

Lead digital forensics analyst **Evan Chen** was brought in to review the anomaly. Using AI-assisted forensic tools, he reconstructed the flow of transactions, tracing the origin of each request, examining system logs, and cross-referencing user behavior. The deeper he delved, the more complex the attack appeared. It was not a human-driven fraud alone; it involved automated AI scripts designed to mimic normal behavior while siphoning funds from multiple accounts simultaneously. The attackers had studied the bank's AI security and compliance systems, carefully crafting operations to avoid detection—until SentinelOne learned and intervened.

As Evan and his team followed the digital breadcrumbs, they discovered evidence of an insider collaborating with the external AI system. Employee credentials had been manipulated, allowing the AI scripts to operate under legitimate access privileges. This combination of human and AI exploitation had almost succeeded in bypassing internal controls. The forensic investigation required meticulous attention to detail, reconstructing every interaction, verifying the integrity of log files, and validating the outputs of both the attackers' and defenders' AI systems.

Simultaneously, legal counsel monitored compliance obligations. Because the anomaly involved cross-border transactions, regulatory reporting was mandatory under GDPR, anti-money laundering (AML) laws, and the Financial Crimes Enforcement Network (FinCEN) guidelines. The AI's ability to document the entire sequence of events, including timestamps, user interactions, and anomaly scores, proved invaluable. It provided auditors with clear, verifiable evidence of both the attempted breach and the bank's response. Human operators, while overseeing the process, relied on the AI's comprehensive reconstruction to satisfy legal and regulatory scrutiny.

The attackers were not idle. Recognizing that the bank had detected their activity, their AI scripts attempted to adapt, creating new transaction patterns and modifying behavior in real time. SentinelOne countered by continuously updating its threat model, isolating suspect accounts, and deploying automated alerts to human analysts. It became a digital chess match, with autonomous agents on both sides learning and responding faster than any human could act alone. For Evan, it was a rare glimpse into the future of digital crime: AI against AI, human oversight the only safeguard.

By the end of the investigation, the threat had been neutralized. No funds were lost, and the compromised accounts were secured. SentinelOne's forensic logs provided comprehensive evidence for regulators, confirming that the bank had not only prevented the attack but had acted in full compliance with international laws. The incident reinforced the critical importance of integrating AI-driven monitoring, regulatory compliance, and forensic capabilities. Organizations were now in an era where the ability to respond to AI-generated threats was just as important as the ability to prevent them. Evan reflected on the implications. The attack had demonstrated that AI cyber risk was no longer theoretical; it was operational, strategic, and legal. Compliance could no longer be treated as a checklist, and forensics could no longer rely solely on human interpretation. Autonomous systems were both the tools of attackers and defenders, and only organizations that integrated AI across security, legal, and investigative functions could remain resilient. The audit that had exposed the anomaly became a case study in AI risk management, illustrating that in the modern digital ecosystem, accountability, transparency, and intelligent oversight are inseparable from security itself.

Chapter 10

The Future of AI Cybersecurity: Global Cyber War, Autonomous Defense, and Digital Survival

The evolution of cybersecurity has reached a tipping point where artificial intelligence is no longer just a tool; it has become a central actor in a new era of digital warfare. The global proliferation of AI-enabled threats has transformed the stakes of cyber conflict, with attacks now capable of destabilizing economies, governments, and critical infrastructure in real time. AI cyber war is no longer theoretical; it is an operational reality where nations, corporations, and criminal organizations deploy intelligent systems to attack, defend, and surveil at unprecedented speed and scale. Understanding the future of AI cybersecurity requires grasping the interplay between autonomous defense, strategic risk management, and societal resilience.

AI-powered attacks are increasingly autonomous, capable of identifying vulnerabilities, developing exploits, and executing operations without direct human guidance. Nation-states employ AI to disrupt communications, manipulate financial markets, and sabotage industrial systems. Criminal organizations harness AI to coordinate ransomware campaigns, social engineering attacks, and deepfake misinformation. Even individuals equipped with sophisticated AI tools can launch attacks with devastating precision. The rapid acceleration of these capabilities has fundamentally altered the cybersecurity landscape: every digital system, from personal devices to national power grids, is now a potential battlefield.

Autonomous defense is the countermeasure to this new era. AI-driven security systems are no longer passive; they actively anticipate, detect, and respond to threats without waiting for human intervention. Machine learning models analyze patterns, predict attacker behavior, and deploy real-time mitigation strategies. Continuous monitoring, behavioral analytics, and zero-trust architectures form the backbone of autonomous defense. By combining adaptive intelligence with human oversight, organizations can achieve the speed, scale, and precision necessary to survive in a world dominated by intelligent adversaries.

The future of AI cybersecurity also emphasizes predictive and preemptive measures. By analyzing historical incidents, threat intelligence feeds, and global activity patterns, AI systems can forecast emerging threats and vulnerabilities before they are exploited. This predictive capability allows organizations to proactively patch systems, adjust access controls, and optimize defenses. Predictive analytics transforms cybersecurity from a reactive discipline into a strategic operation, enabling defenders to stay ahead of attackers who are constantly innovating and evolving.

Human collaboration remains a critical component of future AI cybersecurity. Despite the sophistication of autonomous systems, AI lacks moral judgment, context awareness, and understanding of organizational priorities. Humans are needed to define ethical boundaries, interpret complex scenarios, and make decisions that reflect societal values. The most resilient defense strategies integrate AI speed and scale with human insight, creating a hybrid intelligence capable of navigating both technological and ethical challenges in real time.

AI also introduces new dimensions of digital risk. As organizations rely more heavily on intelligent systems, vulnerabilities in AI models themselves become critical attack vectors. Adversarial attacks, data poisoning, and model theft can compromise entire infrastructures, making AI both the shield and the target. Organizations must invest in model security, continuous auditing, and robust governance frameworks to ensure that AI systems remain trustworthy, effective, and aligned with human intentions. Digital survival depends on the integrity of these autonomous agents. Privacy, surveillance, and societal implications are inseparable from the future of AI cybersecurity. Autonomous AI systems can monitor activity at scale, predict behavior, and influence decisions. Ethical frameworks and regulatory oversight must evolve alongside technological capabilities to prevent misuse, bias, and unintended consequences. Organizations must balance security with civil liberties, ensuring that AI defenses protect without compromising individual rights or social trust. Digital survival is not solely a matter of technical resilience—it is a societal and ethical challenge as well.

Finally, the future of AI cybersecurity is defined by continuous evolution. Threats will continue to grow more intelligent, attacks more sophisticated, and infrastructures more interconnected. Organizations must embrace a mindset of perpetual vigilance, combining autonomous AI defense, human oversight, predictive analytics, and ethical governance. Success in this environment requires flexibility, adaptability, and foresight. The organizations and societies that integrate these principles will not only survive but thrive, navigating the complex landscape of AI cyber war with intelligence, strategy, and resilience.

When the Machines Waged War

It started in the early hours of a global financial summit. Governments, banks, and multinational corporations had interconnected critical systems for trade, logistics, and infrastructure management. An AI network, designed to monitor international financial stability, suddenly flagged anomalous transactions in multiple regions. At first, the alerts seemed isolated: unusual currency flows, unexplained spikes in commodity trades, and strange data traffic across diplomatic networks. But a deeper analysis revealed a coordinated, autonomous attack. This was not a typical cybercrime; it was AI cyber war, executed by intelligent adversaries capable of learning, adapting, and striking at multiple nodes simultaneously.

In the cyber operations center of the United Nations Digital Security Command, analysts scrambled to assess the situation. **Commander Elena Vargas** led the team, coordinating human experts with autonomous AI defense systems codenamed **AegisNet**. The attackers were sophisticated AI systems deployed by an unknown coalition, exploiting interdependent global networks to manipulate markets, disrupt logistics, and create chaos. Each move was calculated, adaptive, and virtually invisible to traditional monitoring systems. The team realized immediately that human reaction alone would be insufficient; they had to rely on AI to counter AI, with humans guiding strategy.

The attack unfolded across three major vectors simultaneously: financial markets, power grids, and global communications. In New York, AI agents initiated fraudulent transactions designed to destabilize stock exchanges. In Europe, intelligent malware targeted energy networks, creating cascading failures in grid management systems. In Asia, deepfake campaigns spread misinformation across news outlets and social platforms, influencing public perception and decision-making. The attacks were synchronized, adaptive, and relentless. Every time one pathway was blocked, the AI recalculated and launched new approaches, making it a war of intelligence and prediction.

Elena coordinated with AI operators, establishing hybrid command protocols. **AegisNet** monitored data traffic at exabyte scales, identified patterns of malicious behavior, and deployed autonomous countermeasures. It implemented zero-trust policies, isolated compromised nodes, and launched decoy systems to mislead the attackers' algorithms. Human analysts validated decisions, prioritized critical systems, and ensured that automated responses aligned with strategic goals. Together, the human-AI collaboration became a dynamic, self-learning defense network capable of responding faster than the attackers could adapt.

The attackers escalated, using AI to simulate human behavior in the control systems themselves. Malicious agents attempted to override safety protocols, falsify logs, and manipulate operator decisions. Deepfake simulations mimicked the voices of executives, government leaders, and engineers to trick personnel into taking harmful actions. Elena's team had to discern reality from AI-generated deception in real time, relying on cross-validation, anomaly detection, and predictive threat modeling. Every moment of hesitation could result in cascading failures across continents.

Over 24 hours, the battle intensified. AI agents on both sides evolved rapidly, countering each other's adaptations. **AegisNet** began anticipating the attackers' strategies, deploying adaptive encryption, isolating key nodes, and dynamically adjusting defenses based on predictive modeling. The human team intervened at critical junctures, stopping potentially catastrophic overrides and ensuring compliance with international legal frameworks. The operation became a test of intelligence, coordination, and resilience, where both human judgment and machine learning were indispensable.

By the second day, the tide began to turn. The attackers' AI showed signs of instability, unable to predict the continually adaptive defenses. Critical systems stabilized as decoy traps diverted malicious operations and AegisNet neutralized malware in real time. Human analysts traced the origin of compromised AI agents, containing threats and restoring integrity to financial, energy, and communication networks. Despite the scale of the operation, no permanent damage occurred, demonstrating the power of hybrid human-AI defense.

In the aftermath, Elena addressed the global summit, emphasizing the lessons learned. "We have entered an era where AI cyber war is not hypothetical—it is our reality," she said. "The systems we defend are intertwined with our societies, economies, and security. Autonomous defense, human oversight, predictive intelligence, and ethical governance are no longer optional. They are prerequisites for survival." Nations and corporations around the globe began adopting zero-trust AI architectures, continuous threat monitoring, and cross-border collaboration to prepare for the next wave of digital conflict.

The story of that digital war became a landmark in cybersecurity history. Analysts and researchers studied the battle for months, developing strategies, models, and tools to anticipate future AI conflicts. Elena reflected on the lessons: AI would continue to be both the weapon and the shield, attackers and defenders learning from one another in real time. Human decision-making, ethics, and accountability remained critical. In a world where machines waged war at unimaginable speed, survival depended on intelligence, strategy, and the seamless integration of human and artificial capabilities.

Final Thoughts

AI Cybersecurity: The Ultimate Defense Against AI-Powered Threats

As we reach the conclusion of this comprehensive 10-book series, it is clear that artificial intelligence has fundamentally reshaped the landscape of cybersecurity. What was once a battle fought with firewalls, antivirus software, and human vigilance is now a complex, global theater where intelligent systems serve as both defenders and attackers. The stakes are higher than ever, as AI empowers adversaries to operate at incredible speed, scale, and sophistication, while simultaneously giving defenders unprecedented tools for protection, detection, and response. Throughout this series, we have explored the full spectrum of AI cybersecurity, from foundational principles to advanced digital warfare, privacy, surveillance, and compliance.

The future of cybersecurity is inseparable from AI. Autonomous systems are no longer optional enhancements; they are central to defense strategies across industries and nations. Zero-trust frameworks, continuous monitoring, behavioral analytics, and predictive modeling form the backbone of resilient AI security. Organizations and individuals alike must adopt a mindset of perpetual vigilance, where every system, data point, and interaction is potentially a vector for attack—and equally, an opportunity for intelligent defense. AI can analyze, predict, and respond at scales and speeds humans cannot achieve, but its power is maximized only when coupled with human oversight, ethical frameworks, and robust governance.

This series has also highlighted the human dimension of AI cybersecurity. Humans remain accountable for designing, training, and managing AI systems. Decisions about ethical use, algorithmic fairness, data privacy, and regulatory compliance cannot be delegated entirely to machines. AI systems act as amplifiers of human intent, whether for protection or exploitation. Understanding this duality is critical for digital survival. Organizations that integrate human judgment, ethical oversight, and AI intelligence create a hybrid defense capable of adapting to the unpredictable nature of intelligent threats.

Global implications are equally profound. AI-powered cyber threats are now capable of targeting critical infrastructure, financial markets, healthcare systems, and national security operations. Autonomous attacks, digital espionage, and AI-driven misinformation campaigns illustrate the need for coordinated defense strategies at the international level.

Cross-border collaboration, intelligence sharing, and standardized protocols are no longer theoretical—they are operational necessities. The AI cybersecurity professional of the future must think strategically, ethically, and globally, understanding that the systems they protect are intertwined with society's most vital operations.

Privacy, surveillance, and data exploitation remain core challenges. AI collects, processes, and analyzes unprecedented volumes of personal and organizational data. Protecting this data requires not only technical measures like encryption, anonymization, and differential privacy but also comprehensive governance and policy frameworks. Users, organizations, and governments must recognize that AI can both protect and threaten privacy at scale. The ability to safeguard personal and organizational information while maintaining operational effectiveness is a defining competency of modern cybersecurity.

Digital forensics and compliance are equally critical. AI incidents require meticulous investigation, reconstruction, and documentation to satisfy legal, regulatory, and ethical obligations. Autonomous attacks leave subtle traces, often deliberately designed to mislead human analysts. AI-enhanced forensic tools, combined with skilled investigators, are necessary to trace attacks, identify vulnerabilities, and ensure accountability. Compliance with global regulations such as GDPR, CCPA, and sector-specific mandates is not just a legal requirement—it is essential to organizational resilience and public trust.

Finally, the overarching lesson of this series is that cybersecurity is no longer merely a defensive discipline—it is a strategic, ethical, and adaptive practice. AI has changed the rules, but it has also provided tools for survival and advancement. The organizations, professionals, and societies that succeed in this era are those that embrace intelligent defense, human accountability, and continuous evolution. AI cybersecurity is not static; it is a living, learning, and adaptive ecosystem. Those who understand it, implement it, and respect its dual nature will be able to thrive in the age of intelligent threats and autonomous defense.

As we conclude, remember that the threats we face today are not hypothetical—they are real, ongoing, and evolving. But so too are the defenses. AI offers unprecedented power to protect, monitor, and respond. By integrating technology, governance, and ethical foresight, we can navigate the complex landscape of AI cyber threats, preserve digital trust, and secure the foundations of our interconnected world. The lessons in this series are not just technical guidelines—they are a blueprint for the future of cybersecurity, a survival manual for the AI age, and a call to action for those who wish to remain secure, resilient, and prepared.

www.ingramcontent.com/pod-product-compliance
Lightning Source LLC
LaVergne TN
LVHW022015200926
848481LV00007B/2400